Amber's Seeing Heart

Joseph Drumheller   Illustrated by   Nataly Simmons

Drumheller Publishing
Spokane, WA USA
josephdrumheller.com

Illustrations and Cover Design: *Nataly Simmons*

Artistic Assistant: *Tamara Zink*

Special Thanks: *Abby B., Cassandra P., Chantelle P., Christine C., Dave and Lynne B., Emily S., Jeanette B., Kathy M., Reinhold W., Ryan G., Sarah D. Tamara Z., Terri M., Tommy M.*

ISBN-10: 1721085297

ISBN-13: 978-1721085293

For All of the
Ambers in this World

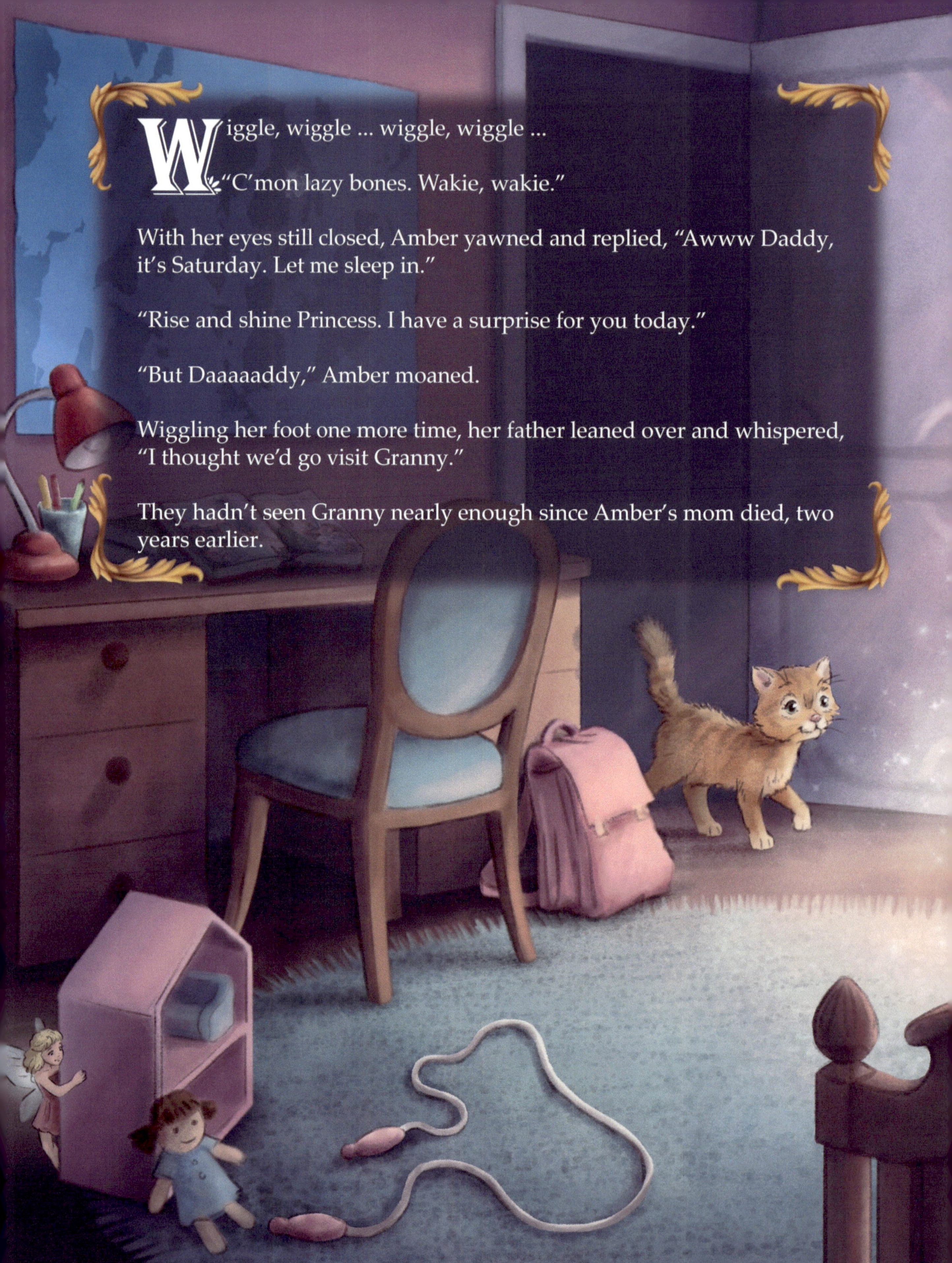

Wiggle, wiggle ... wiggle, wiggle ...

"C'mon lazy bones. Wakie, wakie."

With her eyes still closed, Amber yawned and replied, "Awww Daddy, it's Saturday. Let me sleep in."

"Rise and shine Princess. I have a surprise for you today."

"But Daaaaaddy," Amber moaned.

Wiggling her foot one more time, her father leaned over and whispered, "I thought we'd go visit Granny."

They hadn't seen Granny nearly enough since Amber's mom died, two years earlier.

mber's eyes popped open. "What?!!"

Her father nodded and grinned.

"Yes!" she squealed with delight.

Faster than a jackrabbit, she sprang from her bed and bolted into her closet. Rummaging around in the dark, she quickly dressed herself in mismatched clothes. Seconds later, her little suitcase was packed and wheeling toward the door.

And that's how the journey of a lifetime began.

Granny lived on the most magical island in the Emerald Isle Chain. It was a two-hour ferry ride to get there.

That day, there was a very mysterious fog on the bay. As the ferry pulled away from the dock, her father winked and said, "Looks like there's some extra magic in the air today. What do you think?"

With eyes as big as the moon, Amber nodded and agreed.

About half way into their voyage, rays of sun broke through the lifting fog. The clouds framed a spectacular view of Mt. Marvel in the distance.

Suddenly, someone yelled from the starboard bow, "Whales! Whales! A pod of Orcas!"

It was so beautiful, Amber yelled inn amazement, "Daddy, look!"

The captain slowed the ferry, so passengers could see the Orcas with Mt. Marvel in the background. It was a sight everyone on the ferry would remember for the rest of their lives.

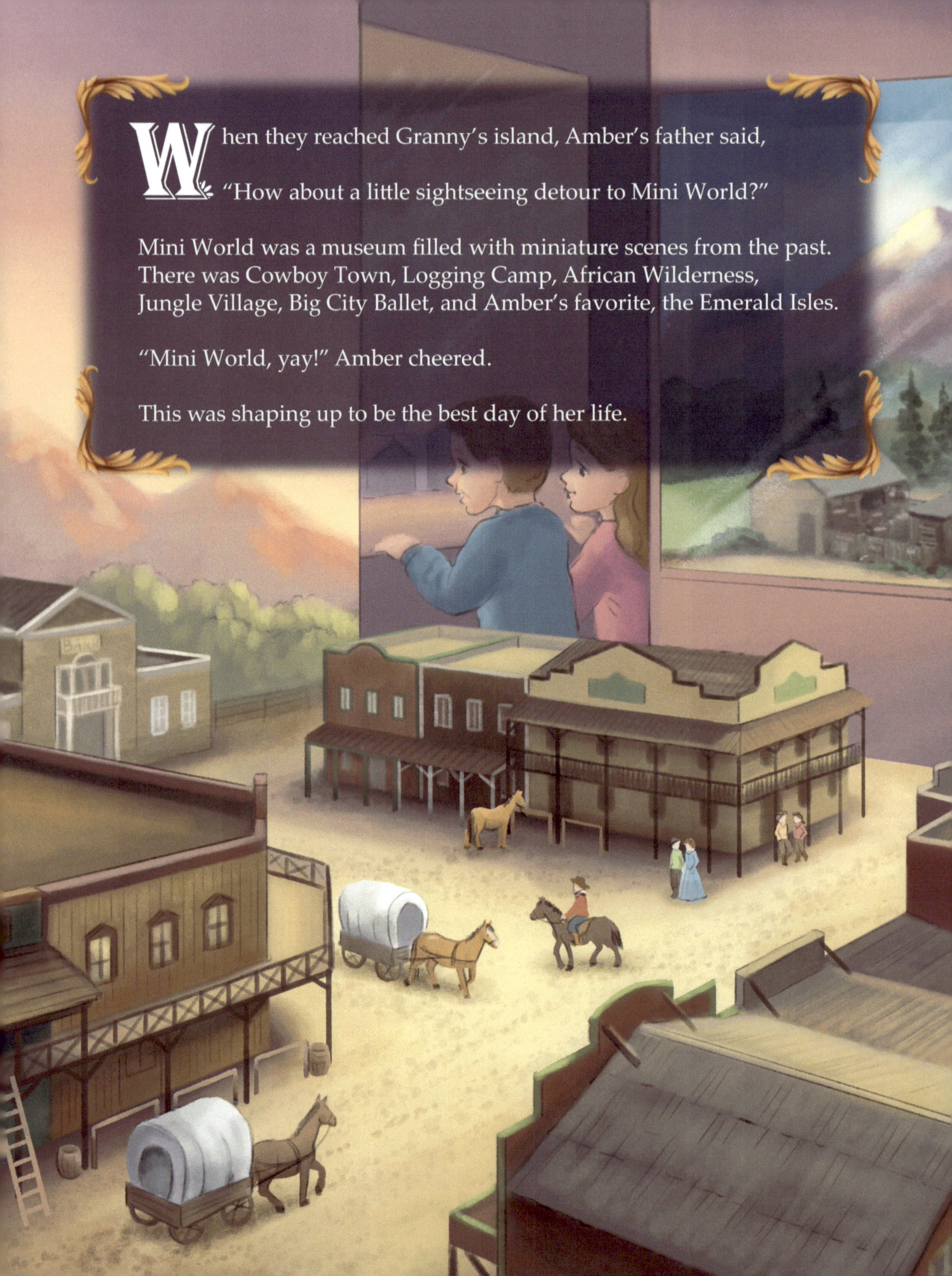

W hen they reached Granny's island, Amber's father said,

"How about a little sightseeing detour to Mini World?"

Mini World was a museum filled with miniature scenes from the past. There was Cowboy Town, Logging Camp, African Wilderness, Jungle Village, Big City Ballet, and Amber's favorite, the Emerald Isles.

"Mini World, yay!" Amber cheered.

This was shaping up to be the best day of her life.

After Mini World, sightseeing continued at Golden Gardens. Amber's favorite flowers were in full bloom. It seemed like all the colors of the rainbow had burst into life.

Next, her father drove to Artist's View at the top of the island, for a majestic overlook of the Emerald Isles. The view of the islands, the sea, and Mt. Marvel was fantastic.

The last stop was Granny's house. Amber was so excited, she felt like she might explode.

Her father pulled to a stop out front. With serious eyes, he looked at Amber and said, "There's something you need to know. Granny had an operation."

Amber's heart sank like a brick. "Is she okay?"

Her father said, "She's alright but she's changed a little. However, one thing hasn't changed; she can't wait to be with you."

With that said, Amber ran like the wind and pounded on Granny's front door.

"Come in!" Granny called.

Amber opened the door and was greeted by the smell of fresh cookies and Granny's cat, Whiskers. After giving Whiskers a quick stroke, Amber dashed to Granny's side.

For the next ten minutes, Amber talked non-stop, telling Granny of all the magical things she had seen that day. When she finally stopped jabbering, she was puzzled and asked, "Granny, why are you wearing sunglasses?"

Granny patted Amber on the head and said, "I had an operation, sweetie. I can't see much any more."

Amber felt horrible. She had just blabbered on and on about beautiful things Granny could no longer see.

"Oh, Granny!" Amber wailed, "I'm so sorry!"

Then she burst into tears.

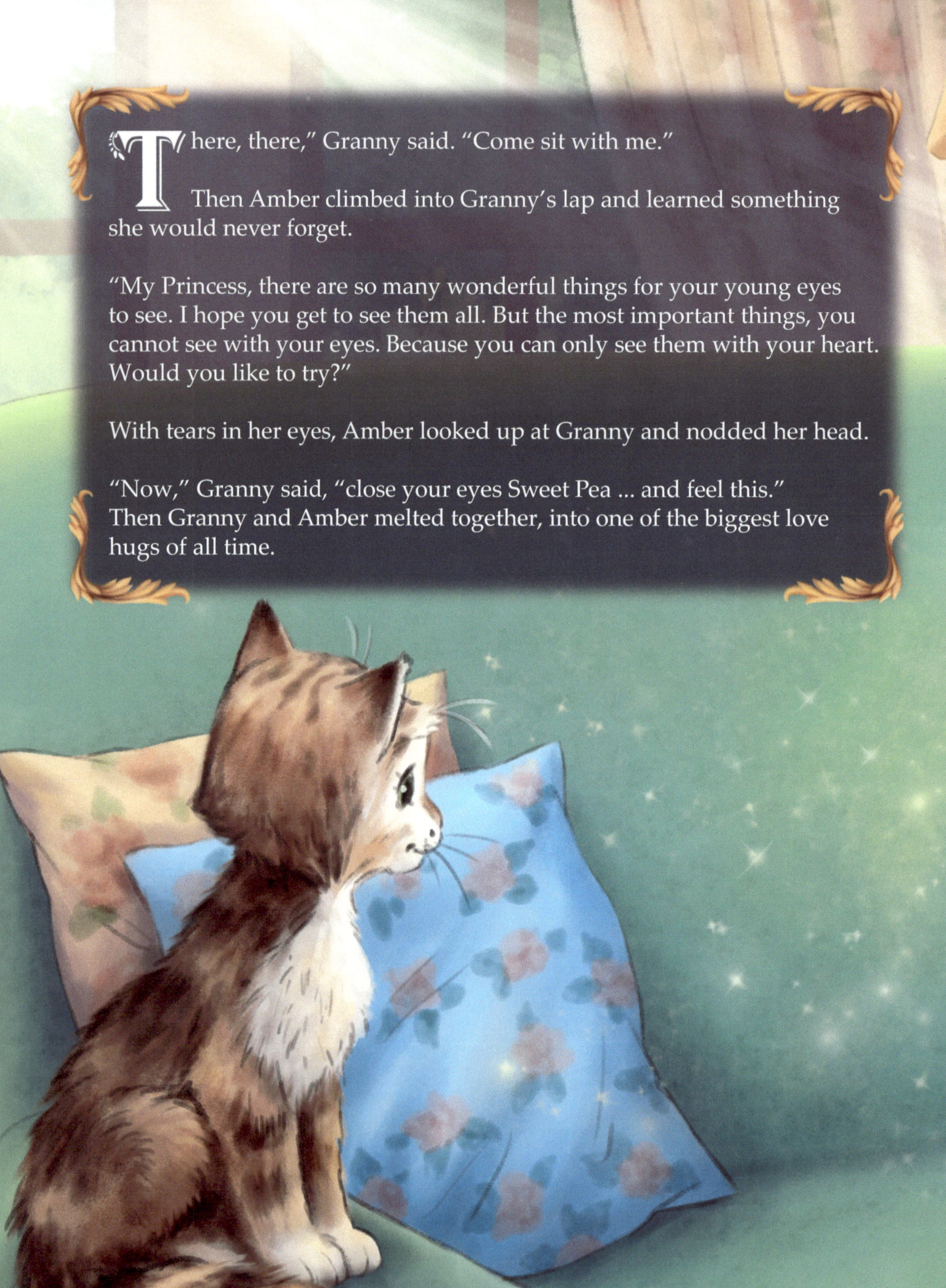

here, there," Granny said. "Come sit with me."

Then Amber climbed into Granny's lap and learned something she would never forget.

"My Princess, there are so many wonderful things for your young eyes to see. I hope you get to see them all. But the most important things, you cannot see with your eyes. Because you can only see them with your heart. Would you like to try?"

With tears in her eyes, Amber looked up at Granny and nodded her head.

"Now," Granny said, "close your eyes Sweet Pea ... and feel this." Then Granny and Amber melted together, into one of the biggest love hugs of all time.

"How was that, Sweetie? Did you feel it in your heart?"
Amber grinned and nodded with a warm glow.

Granny continued. "Now ... think of Whiskers and your Father. Can you still feel it?"

Amber nodded again.

"Good," Granny said. "Now, think of your Mother and let that glow light up your world."

Amber sat still and felt that glow for a good long time. When she finished, Granny said, "Now you know how to see with your heart. You can do it when you get back home."

Amber knew exactly what she meant.

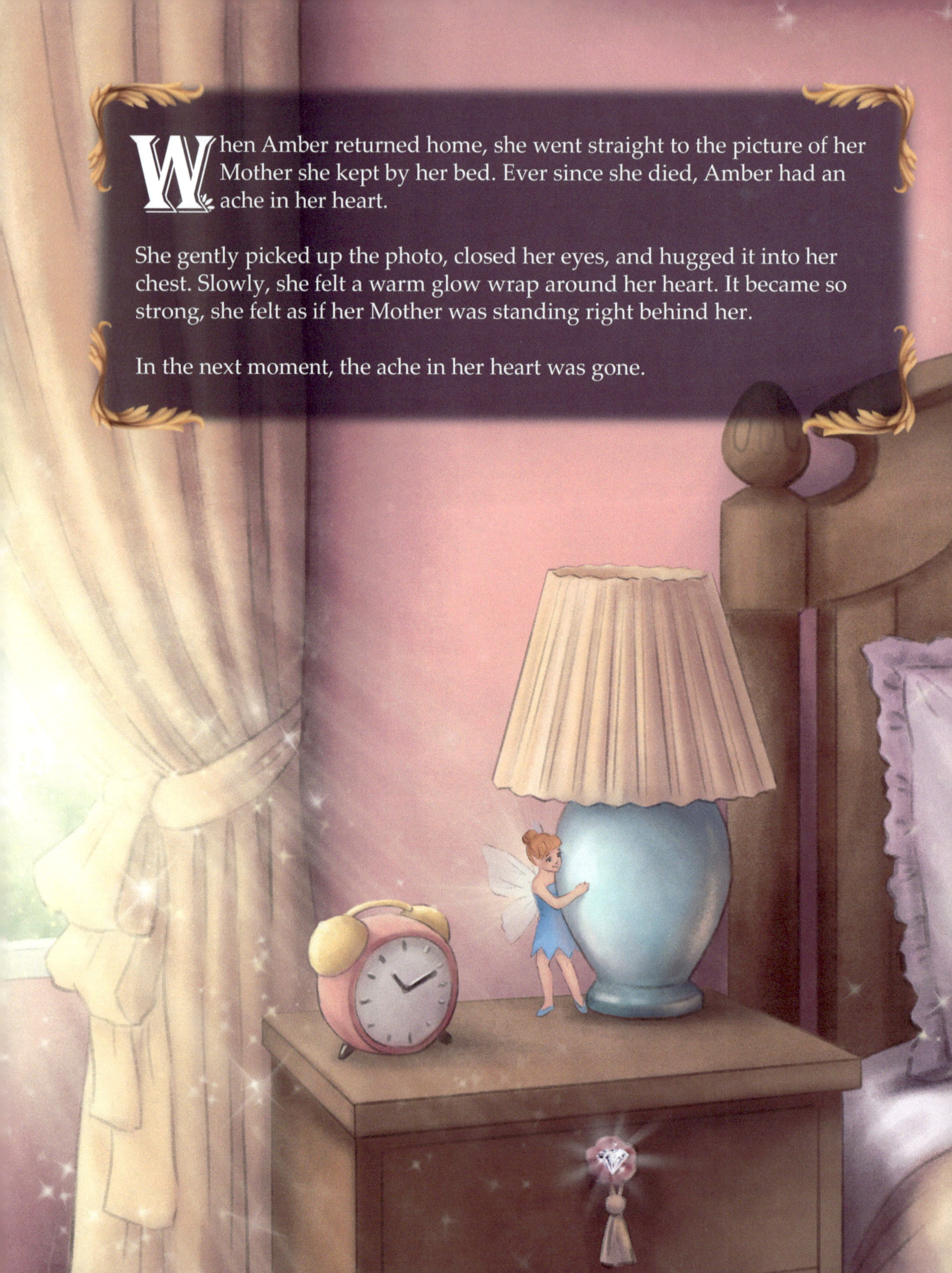

When Amber returned home, she went straight to the picture of her Mother she kept by her bed. Ever since she died, Amber had an ache in her heart.

She gently picked up the photo, closed her eyes, and hugged it into her chest. Slowly, she felt a warm glow wrap around her heart. It became so strong, she felt as if her Mother was standing right behind her.

In the next moment, the ache in her heart was gone.

T hat night, her father read stories and showed Amber pictures of the beautiful things they had seen on their journey. But she closed her eyes and did not look.

Instead, she snuggled deeply into his lap and listened to his gentle voice. Then, she turned her attention to something even more beautiful. It was the love she had for her family.

And that, she saw through the glow of her own heart.

Your Creators

Joseph Drumheller is the author art of more than 30 children's books. He loves to go on site-seeing adventures and then write the story.

Don't tell anybody but he's also Amber's father.

As a child, Nataly Simmons loved exploring new worlds through books so much, she went of to earn a Master's Degree in Art.

Today, she lives her passion, by touching the hearts of children everywhere with her illustrations.

Other Books by Joseph Drumheller

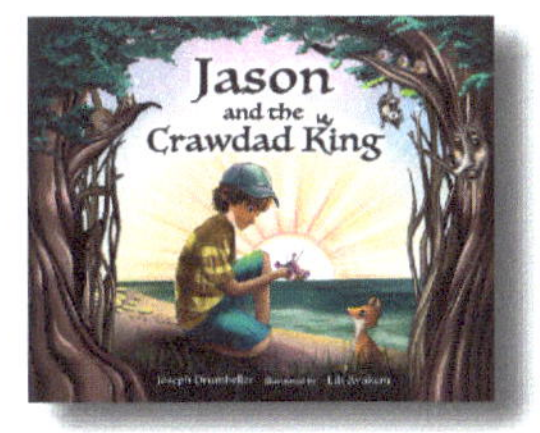

Jason and the Crawdad King

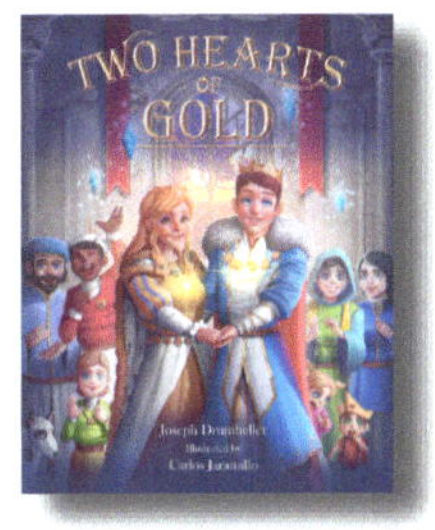

Two Hearts of Gold

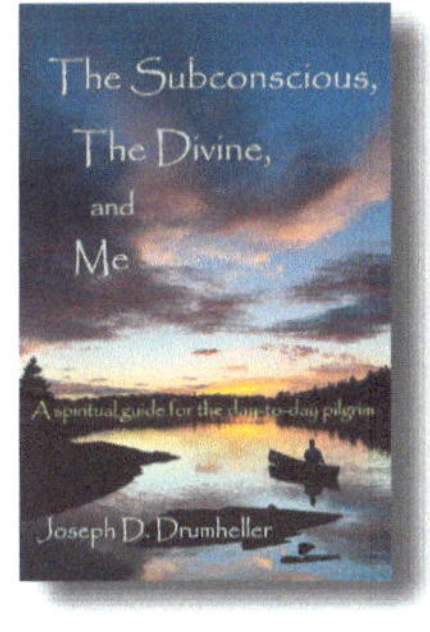

The Subconscious, The Divine and Me

The Unity Oracle
Winner of three literary awards

For books, events, fun, and more:
www.josephdrumheller.com